Teaching College Computer Sciences

Teaching College Computer Sciences

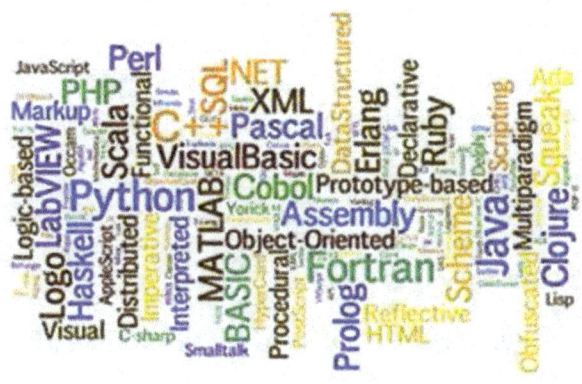

Donald JG Chiarella, PhD, CISM, CDMP

Copyright © Donald JG Chiarella, PhD, CISM, CDMP.

All rights reserved. No part of this book may be reproduced in any form or by any electronic or mechanical means, including information storage and retrieval systems, without permission in writing from the publisher, except by reviewers, who may quote brief passages in a review.

ISBN: 978-1-64826-422-1 (Paperback Edition)
ISBN: 978-1-64826-438-2 (Hardcover Edition)
ISBN: 978-1-64826-406-1 (E-book Edition)

Some characters and events in this book are fictitious. Any similarity to real persons, living or dead, is coincidental and not intended by the author.

Book Ordering Information

Phone Number: 347-901-4929 or 347-901-4920
Email: info@globalsummithouse.com
Global Summit House
www.globalsummithouse.com

Printed in the United States of America

FORWARD

I wanted to write a book to help other teachers and students see how it can be done by a regular person. I never thought I would teach college computers sciences until I actually started to in my job. I was not concerned with others learning abilities nor did I dive into this job blindly. I had always been a good student in high school but never took any computer courses there. I was more interested in sports than my academics at the time. It took some weaning but I finished undergraduate school with a nice GPA after I stopped playing sports. I spent more time at the computer science center and raised my GPA. I felt this was the sure thing to do and I would get a good job. Back in those days computer time on the time sharing mainframe was at a premium. There were no PC labs. If you dropped your punch card deck you were out of luck. By the time I had my first computer job I had mastered several languages and had confidence in my abilities. I did not know I would evolve as I learned more languages and a database approach I became a pretty good DBA who could write applications and perform maintenance on systems and operating systems. The chances I had with the Navy to excel were outstanding as a building block to my career. Now that I have CISO understanding I am truly prepared to lead others. I hope you enjoy this book and can find it useful to your career. Keep on trying hard and preparing through better technology and management training.

Don

CONTENTS

Forward v

1. Why start teaching? 1
2. Try High School first 3
3. Community Colleges 5
4. So you have the passion 8
5. They pay you to learn more 12
6. Computer Lab 15
7. Internet teaching 18
8. Distance Education 19
9. Undergraduates 29
10. Graduates 31
11. Teaching to the textbook 32
12. Teaching the Software Development Life Cycle 34
13. Teaching projects 36
14. Trace of Courses 41
15. A Sample Syllabus Template 45
16. A Sample Research Paper Template 49
17. Grading online 51
18. Evaluating programs 53
19. Student evaluations 54
20. The Greatest Teachers 55
21. Adjunct forever? 57
22. Job Hunting 59
23. Flexibility 61
24. Adjunct Benefits 63
25. Final Thoughts 65
26. Bibliography 67
27. Biography 68

1
WHY START TEACHING?

For me the start was semi-religious. I was 27 and I was assigned to teach Natural Programming to Naval Executives. I was an unlikely teacher but I enjoyed helping others and I was finishing my masters degree at American University in Technology of Management. I obtained a part time[1] teaching job with EZ Method Driving School and taught Drivers Ed for two semesters to high schoolers in PG County. I did not know then that I would have an experience at Cheltenham United Methodist Church that would change me forever. My wife and I volunteered to teach Sunday School at church. Our kids were in the class. I wanted to see how good my wife was as she is a professional teacher. She did not disappoint me. We had a great little class and I learned a few things from her. I felt really good that I could teach what I learned in Sunday school all those years before. It gave me confidence I never had before. God had led me into this work through the back door. After that Sunday school class I signed up to teach community college computer science courses and got the job at Charles Community College[2] in Southern Maryland. At first I taught Introductory courses but soon I was teaching more advanced courses. I was asked to teach undergraduate courses at UMUC and

---

[1] I was a GS-11 Civil Servant for the Navy at the time.
[2] Now known as College of Southern Maryland in Mitchellville Maryland just south of St Charles.

I accepted. Over the next 15 years I taught 17 courses for UMUC[3] while still working for community colleges too. This was while I worked my regular daytime job. I always felt I was enhancing my daytime job. I never knew that I would grow into a lifelong adjunct faculty member with no benefits. The only benefit was knowing you helped others. I have tried to get full time tenured positions but always failed since I have a regular job for the state.

The picture below is one of Grace Hopper, the first woman programmer. She worked for the Navy as well as Harvard. I met her twice at Navy Medical. She was a dynamic lecturer and always positive about computer sciences. She helped invent early COBOL compilers. She was funny and spoke very good concerning computer careers. She coined the term computer "bug" from a moth stuck in the vacuum tubes of an early computer. She reached the Naval rank of Rear Admiral and was well respected.

Grace Hopper

---

[3] UMUC rehired me 3 times but I never left.

2
TRY HIGH SCHOOL FIRST

You might not think you can teach but you have an advantage over high school students. You graduated years ago and have some wisdom about how to get there even if you are only in your twenties . All you need is the students and right course to teach them. In my case, drivers education was needed by all the kids and they knew I would not flunk them all. This did not stop them from being teenagers. They were unruly and lacked appreciation of the fact that they would crash someday and need my help. Most of them were cocky and arrogant. It could never happen to them. I proceeded to tell them my stories and how I crashed one of my cars[4]. So the class helped me as well as them. High school students taking drivers education only see the good things. You have to force the bad things on them to scare them some what. We had films that did that. I used a book called <u>The Courteous Driver</u>.

"He abdicated his throne and got into software."

---

[4]   I felt this class turned me around to being a much safer driver.

I did not teach them to drive in a car even though I had driven several of my cars and my motorcycles by this time. My class was the 30 hours before their actual 6 hour driving class. They needed 80% on tests to pass the course. So I had to make them aware of the rules and regulations of the highway. It was a challenge in that many of them acted like they knew everything before they got to class. What I gained was that I did not like teaching high school students in the Washington DC suburbs. I found them disruptive and rude to each other. I could barely control them. They were in my class because the school system did not teach driver's education any more. This was a tragedy because real teachers could get extra cash teaching this stuff. They also knew the way to discipline the kids. I had to learn fast. The parents paid extra for the Drivers Education so I knew I had an advantage over the kids. Most of them tried to learn but I think the best teacher is behind the wheel experience. I did my best to get them there with some information beforehand. It was not a teacher's dream job but it was teaching. And it was part time income. This course taught me that I could teach but that high school was probably not where I wanted to focus my attention. The kids just seemed too immature even if I did like them. Years later MVA came up with the graduated licensing program and this program probably has saved a lot of young lives. Delaying driving until the later years when they are more mature is a good idea. For most teenagers driving is the first grown up thing they are asked to do. Driving at age 16 with no previous experience is like carrying a loaded gun. Statistics show that more kids get into accidents than older age groups. Maybe they need an early accident and a do over to get it out of the way. This is the only way they will earn the true value of safe driving. The gory crash films did not do it most of the time.

3

COMMUNITY COLLEGES

When I started teaching at Community College I knew all the students wanted to be there and paid to be there. I also knew they would behave better than my Driver's Ed classes. I expected more from them on day one. My first class was Introduction to Computers and I had some older people in the class who did not know anything about computers. By that time in 1989 the PC revolution had started and people needed more information about PC applications like Word Processing and databases. I had mainframe experience and micro experience on all the software from my days at Navy Medical. Teaching these folks was easy for me. I stretched my liking of the field by teaching this class. Since it came after my Epiphany teaching at Cheltenham UMC with my wife I knew I was suppose to be there. I had earned my masters degree in early 1988 so I had enough education to teach well. It was fresh in my mind at the time and the technology was changing. I was young enough to stay up with the changes and help others learn new stuff.

My second community college job came at Catonsville Community College working for Frank White in the Business Computing Department in 1991. His wife taught COBOL. I was an ex-COBOL programmer so I knew how to teach that but I was assigned to networks and databases. This was easy again because I had training in both these areas and had been a mainframe systems engineer. By 1991 I had returned to the Federal Government and was managing a LAN network using Netware 386. I was still learning more about computer languages like Dbase and Clipper. These were my strong suits as a computer specialist. But I also knew how to write books and had completed my first book by 1991 for WH&O in Massachusetts. It was a book on <u>NATURAL Prototyping</u>. NATURAL is a language similar to COBOL and FORTRAN mixed together. It is a 4GL. That first book sold a lot of copies here and in the UK. I received $2500 for the book. I was still on staff at UMUC but worked whenever I had a chance.

In 1993, I worked at Anne Arundel Community College for my first time. It was a large school and fed students into University of Maryland College Park where I attended. I taught an Introductory Course but was ready for upper level courses.

In 2002, I taught at AACC again and opened Arundel Mills. I taught Data Communications in a 200 level course for 2 semesters. It was a lab course. I enjoyed teaching there and had fun with the students. Some of them worked for NSA and some of them worked for other government agencies. I was learning from them as I taught the classes. The most important thing I took away was the fact that many of the students were interested in what I thought rather than what the book said. They asked me to write a book for the class so I did. I have kept it to assign as a supplemental text next time I teach that course. It is called <u>Modern Communications Systems</u> and is offered on Amazon.com.

In 2012, I will again work at AACC if I am assigned a position. The adjunct faculty handler has met with me and said he would be interested in hiring me in Spring of 2012 if he has an opening. I am not holding my breath. I am old enough to know the realities.

Donald Knuth and the Art of Computer Programming is required reading for computer scientists and computer science majors. In my case I was a Management Information Systems Major and this was another term for programmer or systems engineer. I found the Knuth book when I was a Supervisory DBA. The book is like a standard among programmers and computer science teachers. Knuth won an award for the book. It comes in a series of volumes.

4

SO YOU HAVE THE PASSION

If you have the passion you can do anything. This really applies to teaching. There is no better feeling than knowing you have helped someone learn something. This is exciting and every time feels like a million. If you capture the passion you feel for this you have done something good. That will drive you to greatness in your lifetime. I feel it has helped me in my daily life as well as my professional life. It has led me to charity work for the Masonic lodge and church. It has been a great awakening in my soul. How do you know if you have the passion to teach? When you enjoy working with younger people and informing them of principles of your work then you know you are ready. When it is a joy to share your life.

Computer sciences is like a light in someone's mind. Once you see the light turn on you get really good satisfaction from that experience. People think it is too hard. But making it simple for the masses is an art form. Students always think they can do the work when they are challenged and led in the right direction. Lab courses are the best because you can be right there showing them how to do the programming. This is the best feature about computer sciences courses. I knew I wanted to program once I took FORTRAN and did all the programs for the 10 projects on my own. I want all my students to have that same epiphany when they take my courses. There is a lot of money in programming if you are good. The passion helps you be the best you can be. Teaching computer sciences has helped me as a supervisor also. I know how to train people so I do not waste time on trivial stuff when I can get them educated. Some programmers have plenty of confidence and no talent. Some have great talent and no confidence. You have to adjust your lectures to help them all. Building skills is the number one job of the supervisor and computer teacher. Doing it with passion is beyond compare.

If you write software you need to read Weinberg's book. This will help you understand why you think the way you do as a programmer.

As you branch out into various classes in computers sciences you become more well rounded. Teaching Data Communications was very different from Relational Databases and required more thought on how to provide useful software training. I think I learned more than my share. Tele-working to websites and mentoring online students was a great environment for me. Students who learned to listen online became the best writers and I evaluated them better than those who did not write well. Using the software of the online classroom they got used to distance education. They became better students and more familiar with technologies and computers. I had several students who were managers and were in graduate school part time. They really had good online writing abilities and showed me what they knew in every assignment. They usually had no problems with the assignments in the textbooks. I wanted them to go beyond the textbooks and apply the information to their work. Many of them did this very well. They surprised me with their enthusiasm and work ethics. Just when I thought they could not hang with me they surpassed my expectations. I always learned more from the students then they learned from me. Each one of them had critical information about new job fields that i did not know about. Through good writing and communications they showed me they had learned the materials and what data communications could do for the average citizen. They were netizens with a reason for online computing. I really enjoyed them for my five years of graduate teaching Data Communications 651 at Aspen University.

I became passionate about Distance Education and am still hopeful that this is the way of the future. Many people will be able to attend college because of this method. And it is customized to the working adult. Even now I long for more online Center for Homeland Defense training both as student and teacher. It is most effective in bring training goals to mind. For an old Navy computer specialist I would have it no other way. The passion is still there after 35 years although now it is channeled into cyber security and online training. Blackboard is the best online environment I have seen and used. This was used at GW and Ashford Universities[5]. It surpasses the others – webtycho and webct. Moodle is the best video display system online. This was used at Naval Post Graduate School[6] online training recently in Homeland Security. This is a free program of online courses.

---

[5] Ashford University is located in Iowa. A small NAIA school with a good online reputation.

[6] NPS - Center for Homeland Defense at www.nps.edu

5

THEY PAY YOU TO LEARN MORE

As long as they pay you to learn more how can you bypass that opportunity? The fun is that while you learn you also teach. It is a cycle worthy of notice to most people in computer sciences. It is our understanding of social sciences and people that increases our managerial abilities. This cross between social sciences and hard sciences has always worked well for me. Learning more in different areas makes you broader and you should try this instead of an upward or deep focus all the time. By paying me to learn more the government has made me a better employee and supervisor. My last degree was paid for by my employer and I learned a lot about managing people. It was not a technical degree at all. The amount of work was similar to many technical courses and even less than many. But the ideas were major and they even spanned politics. Organizational management is concerned with many aspects of where we are going strategically. Who would not want to get paid for learning? The college teacher knows this secret. If he teaches he will learn more and get paid. What a deal?

Now my employer will pay for an MBA[7]. I feel fortunate that they want me to go for the goals. I am an expert in online education at SHA.

---

[7] I am cautious about this statement as previous employers have reneged on their tuition reimbursement agreements when they saw I was ready to finish the programs. I paid out of pocket to finish courses in both programs.

I can offer advice to teachers and course designers as well as students. The best online education is coming from schools using blackboard environments with teachers monitoring the web environment and class projects and assignments. Blackboard allows student discussion groups and the teacher can monitor all the threads.

How much education is enough? How smart is smart enough? The traditional 3 degree system is flawed in my opinion. It does not make you broader only deeper. Consider Solomon the wisest man of all time. First off you ask for wisdom in your prayers not wealth. Solomon was granted wisdom above all men. For this he had 700 wives which helped trade relations with all these countries. It was determined by God that his wives corrupted him from his own religion into theirs. The prophets said Solomon was to lose his kingdom to his builder of the Temple Jereboam. Solomon's son Reheboam received Judah to rule over and Jereboam received all the other tribes of Israel. So if the wisest of all men made mistakes how can we avoid them? Solomon thought he was honoring the other religions. He thought he had the wisdom to promote them without interfering in his own religion and thus reducing conflict. He taxed his countrymen even after the temple was built and lost control of common people. Seems Solomon had his problems even with Devine wisdom granted to him. He left his legacy to the Masonic Lodge and to this day they use him as an example for wisdom and truth above worldly wealth. Solomon did not go to college. The college system was created by the Greeks. We specialize in areas that are subdivided by the colleges. This is the western style of education. But suppose we went sideways like Solomon instead of deeper? Would we not learn more in fewer days? Starting all over again in each of the areas of specialty is hard and demands a new view of wisdom and learning abilities. In fact, Solomon realized that there were many religions of the world and they may all be very similar. He was granted the highest wisdom by his God. By exposing himself to new Gods and religions of his wives he saw what many others saw. There are many religions and many Gods. This is a fact not withstanding his belief in the God of Israel.

We have to look to new ways of learning in order to learn more. When we are paid to learn we look in logical places for education. We stay in the ordered academic world. When we are paid to learn we are bound to give back a dividend of new ideas. This is what Solomon did and he was punished for it. Not saying it was wrong just saying you have to be unafraid to break the mould if you are truly expecting to be educated in many areas of specialty that compliment each other. An example would be the lawyer who went to law school and medical school and practiced as a medical doctor. He would be most valuable in legal cases involving doctors. Each life job we have trains us for future greatness and wisdom. Every president must have certain life experiences before he is given a chance to run our country. The more varied the experiences the better. The better the education the better president we get. This is why the founding fathers said the president must be at least 35 years old in the US constitution.

You never stop learning in all your life. This is why you have to always find more challenging work. Even ex-presidents have to find better work where they can impact the world. We experience everything in sequence and different for each of us. The more we learn the more we experience new things and make them better. More degrees means more knowledge and this is a noble goal that Solomon would have appreciated.

6
COMPUTER LAB

If you have ever been a network manager then you know computer lab can be an excellent experience for the students. You can show them the tricks of the trade online and get them to execute software utilities after you try them on the overhead. This is powerful. I even loaded a server for the students in one lab. They liked that class.

You can play around online and loosen up the students attitudes towards computing. You can teach online web building. You can teach surfing the websites with software. You can teach them to program in HTML. There are endless things you can do online that you can not do offline in a textbook. You can even put all your class notes into a power point slide set and show them new stuff every week in Blackboard. You prearrange all your tests and exams and assignments and then you sit back and deliver the class. It is really the next best thing in programming your class. The grading is automatic for tests. You give participation grades.

Computer labs can also be great for teaching any type of computer sciences course. I have taught Data Communications and Cybersecurity this way. They were both done with overheads. The text was only used as a reference offline. I think the students get more out of these classes that are hands on. You still teach major concepts on the blackboard but you move along into software faster. They understand the connection between concepts and real world applications better because you can immediately show them the technical side of what you are explaining. This is lost in many off line courses.

Teaching Oracle and PL/SQL online is ideal for the students. In a lab class like this you can try all the different combinations of commands and populate the database tables. Oracle commands can be explored and used at the will of the student. Good examples need to be designed to run through all the command types. We did this at SHA and the class was a success with more than 30 graduates. The network administrator provided us with a computer lab of computers. He supported the lab during the class time and made it worthwhile for everyone. It was not easy to find extra computers for the lab but we did it. It brought out the idea that we should have a permanent computer lab for training.

There is a cost for computer labs and only the newest facilities can afford them. I would say that the older schools have a hard time adapting to newer computer facilities. This must be judged by the students before they enroll in the programs. It is possible to get a tour of the computer facility before you take classes there. I would insist upon this so you get the best training available. I have taught at major universities who always had the resources we needed for lab courses so I think I have taken this fact for granted. Smaller schools may have limited budgets for technology. For the most part, it is common knowledge that technology has driven new advances in computer labs that we are talking about. With large community college and universities there should be no problem getting the technology you need in the classroom computer lab.

If you are teaching a lab course, you need to know the network administrator at the school where you are teaching. This can be a loose relationship but it needs to be there in case you need support. Do not try to let the network administrator know you have done his job already. You need him as an ally to teach your students at all times.

7

INTERNET TEACHING

In the schools I have taught, one was done totally online on internet at the schools website. This was graduate program and I taught each student independently one at a time for $100 a student. It was not as effective as the computer lab but was not a total wash out either. Each student proved to me over the semester that they could use online software to read home works and turn in assignments. We had online discussions but they were not as logical as in Blackboard discussion groups. I would check for activity every day at noon. If students had done their next assignment they could move onto more advanced material. I graded them as they turned in assignments and they could see their grades. They followed a book and did the questions in the back of each chapter which were also graded. I had a copy of the master book and the answer key. The book was <u>Business Data Communications</u> by William Stallings. This book won an MIT award for college textbooks. It was really good. It made my job easier than ever before. The student was expected to read and do the home works for 10 weeks. After 10 weeks they were given a final exam which was also graded immediately. Then a final grade was computed and recorded for each student. Most students liked this format. I found it was not as good as computer labs. I was merely a facilitator not a teacher. It was on the students to put the effort into the class. If they had problems reading then they would fail. I always felt this was unacceptable.

8
DISTANCE EDUCATION

Traditionally in the United States Distance Education started in the 1930s. Back then it was done by correspondence courses. My dad attended Cleveland Institute of Electronics while he served in the US Air Force. He turned his homework in by mailing the test booklet back to the school. Today, this school is still teaching Electronics and Computers. It must have been good because my dad worked for Air Force One avionics division and led some other technical radar guys. When he got out he went to work for Pax River NAS STRIKE and worked on Naval Aircraft. I watched as he completed his red workbooks and sent them to the school. I was still in high school at the time and I did not realize it was like a college. The DETC (Distance Education Training Council) certified schools are listed on the website of the US Department of Education. These schools have the most experience with distance education even before the computer.

Name	Category	City	State	WebSite
Abraham Lincoln University	Degree Granting	Los Angeles	CA	http://www.alu.edu
Aerobics and Fitness Association of America (AFAA)	Postsecondary	Sherman Oaks	CA	http://www.afaa.com
Allied American University	Degree Granting	Laguna Hills	CA	http://www.allied.edu
Allied Business Schools, Inc.	Postsecondary	Laguna Hills	CA	http://www.alliedschools.com
Allied National High School	High School	Laguna Hills	CA	http://www.alliedhighschool.com
Allied Schools	Postsecondary	Laguna Hills	CA	http://www.alliedschools.com
American College of Healthcare Sciences	Degree Granting	Portland	OR	http://www.achs.edu
American College of Technology	Degree Granting	Saint Joseph	MO	http://www.acot.edu
American Graduate School of Education	Degree Granting	Tempe	AZ	http://www.agse.edu
American Graduate University	Degree Granting	Covina	CA	http://www.agu.edu
American Health Information Management Association	Postsecondary	Chicago	IL	http://campus.ahima.org
American Institute of Applied Science	Postsecondary	Youngsville	NC	http://www.aiasinc.com
American Military University	Degree Granting	Charles Town	WV	http://www.amu.apus.edu

American Public University	Degree Granting	Charles Town	WV	http://www.apu.apus.edu
American Public University System (see American Public University and American Military University)	Degree Granting	Charles Town	WV	http://www.apus.edu/
American Sentinel University	Degree Granting	Aurora	CO	http://www.americansentinel.edu
Anaheim University	Degree Granting	Anaheim	CA	http://www.anaheim.edu
Antioch School of Church Planting and Leadership Development	Degree Granting	Ames	IA	http://www.antiochschool.edu
Applied Professional Training, Inc.	Degree Granting	Carlsbad	CA	http://www.aptc.edu
Army Institute for Professional Development (ATIC-SDL)	Military	Fort Eustis	VA	https://www.atrrs.army.mil/atrrscc
Art Instruction Schools	Postsecondary	Minneapolis	MN	http://www.artinstructionschools.edu
Ashworth College	Degree Granting	Norcross	GA	http://www.ashworthcollege.edu
Ashworth College Career Diploma (Formerly Professional Career Development Institute)	Postsecondary	Norcross	GA	http://www.ashworthcollege.edu
Aspen University	Degree Granting	Denver	CO	http://www.aspen.edu

Name	Type	City	State	URL
At-Home Professions (a division of Weston Distance Learning)	Postsecondary	Fort Collins	CO	http://www.at-homeprofessions.edu
Atlantic University	Degree Granting	Virginia Beach	VA	http://www.atlanticuniv.edu
Avondale & Williams Preparatory High School	High School	Scranton	PA	http://www.pennfosterhighschool.com
Babel University Professional School of Translation (HI)	Degree Granting	Honolulu	HI	http://www.babel.edu
Blackstone Career Institute	Postsecondary	Allentown	PA	http://www.blackstone.edu
Brigham Young University Independent Study	High School	Provo	UT	http://elearn.byu.edu
Brighton College	Postsecondary	Scottsdale	AZ	http://www.brightoncollege.edu
California Coast University	Degree Granting	Santa Ana	CA	http://www.calcoast.edu
California Intercontinental University	Degree Granting	Diamond Bar	CA	http://www.caluniversity.edu
California Miramar University	Degree Granting	San Diego	CA	http://www.calmu.edu
California National University for Advanced Studies	Degree Granting	Northridge	CA	http://www.cnuas.edu
California Southern University	Degree Granting	Irvine	CA	http://www.calsouthern.edu
Catholic Distance University	Degree Granting	Hamilton	VA	http://www.cdu.edu

Childcare Education Institute	Postsecondary	Duluth	GA	http://www.cceionline.edu
Citizens' High School	High School	Orange Park	FL	http://www.citizenshighschool.com
City Vision College	Degree Granting	Kansas City	MO	http://www.cityvision.edu
Cleveland Institute of Electronics, Inc.	Degree Granting	Cleveland	OH	http://www.cie-wc.edu
Columbia Southern University	Degree Granting	Orange Beach	AL	http://www.columbiasouthern.edu
Concord Law School of Kaplan University	Degree Granting	Los Angeles	CA	http://info.concordlawschool.edu
Deakin University (Australia)	Degree Granting	Geelong	VC	http://www.deakin.edu.au
Diamond Council of America	Postsecondary	Nashville	TN	http://www.diamondcouncil.org
Dunlap-Stone University	Degree Granting	Phoenix	AZ	http://www.dunlap-stone.edu
Ellis University	Degree Granting	Chicago	IL	http://www.ellis.edu
Gemological Institute of America	Postsecondary	Carlsbad	CA	http://www.gia.edu
Global University	Degree Granting	Springfield	MO	http://www.globaluniversity.edu
Grantham University	Degree Granting	Kansas City	MO	http://www.grantham.edu
Griggs International Academy	High School	Berren Springs	MI	http://www.griggs.edu
Griggs University	Degree Granting	Berren Springs	MI	http://www.griggs.edu
Hadley School for the Blind	Postsecondary	Winnetka	IL	http://www.hadley.edu

Harrison Middleton University	Degree Granting	Tempe	AZ	http://www.hmu.edu
Henley-Putnam University	Degree Granting	San Jose	CA	http://www.henley-putnam.edu
Holmes Institute	Degree Granting	Golden	CO	http://www.holmesinstitute.org
Humanities and Sciences Academy (AZ)	High School	Tempe	AZ	http://www.humsci.org
Humanities and Sciences Academy (IL)	High School	Chicago	IL	http://www.humscionline.org
Humanities and Sciences Academy of the United States	High School	Tempe	AZ	http://www.humsci.org
Huntington College of Health Sciences	Degree Granting	Knoxville	TN	http://www.hchs.edu
Hypnosis Motivation Institute	Postsecondary	Tarzana	CA	http://www.hypnosis.edu
ICI University	Degree Granting	Springfield	MO	http://www.globaluniversity.edu
ICS Canada	Postsecondary	Westmount	QC	http://www.icslearn.ca
INSTE Bible College	Degree Granting	Ankeny	IA	http://www.inste.edu
Institute of Logistical Management	Postsecondary	Burlington	NJ	http://www.mylogisticscareer.com
International Commerce Secondary Schools	High School	Phoenix	AZ	http://www.humsci.org
International Import-Export Institute (see Dunlap-Stone University)	Degree Granting	Phoenix	AZ	http://iiei.dunlap-stone.edu

International Sports Sciences Association	Postsecondary	Carpinteria	CA	http://www.issaonline.edu
ISSA	Postsecondary	Carpinteria	CA	http://www.issaonline.edu
James Madison High School	High School	Norcross	GA	http://www.ashworthcollege.edu
Kona University	Degree Granting	Kailua-Kona	HI	http://www.kona.edu
Lakewood College	Postsecondary	Lakewood	OH	http://www.accri.org
Marine Corps Institute	Military	Washington Navy Yard	DC	http://www.mci.usmc.mil
Martinsburg Institute	Degree Granting	Martinsburg	WV	http://www.martinsburginstitute.edu
McKinley College (A Division of Weston Distance Learning, Inc.)	Degree Granting	Fort Collins	CO	http://www.mckinleycollege.edu
Milburn High School Online	High School	Woodbridge	VA	http://www.milburnonline.org
National Paralegal College	Degree Granting	Phoenix	AZ	http://nationalparalegal.edu
National Tax Training School	Postsecondary	Mahwah	NJ	http://www.nattax.com
National Training, Inc.	Postsecondary	Orange Park	FL	http://www.nationaltrainingschools.com/
National Training, Inc. Training Site	Postsecondary	Green Cove Springs	FL	http://www.nationaltrainingschools.com
New Charter University	Degree Granting	Birmingham	AL	http://www.new.edu
New Learning Resources Online	High School	Jackson	MS	http://www.nlro.org
New York Institute of Photography	Postsecondary	New York	NY	http://www.nyip.com

Name	Type	City	State	URL
Northwest Institute of Literary Arts	Degree Granting	Freeland	WA	http://www.nila.edu
Paralegal Institute	Degree Granting	Scottsdale	AZ	http://www.theparalegalinstitute.edu
Penn Foster Career School	Postsecondary	Scranton	PA	http://www.pennfoster.edu
Penn Foster College	Degree Granting	Scottsdale	AZ	http://www.pennfostercollege.edu
Penn Foster High School	High School	Scranton	PA	http://www.pennfosterhighschool.com
Perelandra College	Degree Granting	La Mesa	CA	http://www.perelandra.edu
Rhodec International	Postsecondary	Quincy	MA	http://www.Rhodec.edu
Seminario Biblico INSTE (See INSTE Bible College)	Degree Granting	Ankeny	IA	http://www.inste.edu
Seminary Extension Independent Study Institute	Postsecondary	Nashville	TN	http://www.seminaryextension.org
Sessions College for Professional Design	Degree Granting	Tempe	AZ	http://www.sessions.edu
Sheffield School of Interior Design	Postsecondary	New York	NY	http://www.sheffield.edu
Sonoran Desert Institute	Degree Granting	Scottsdale	AZ	http://www.sdi.edu
Southwest University	Degree Granting	Kenner	LA	http://www.southwest.edu
Taft Law School	Degree Granting	Santa Ana	CA	http://www.TaftU.edu
Teacher Education University	Degree Granting	Winter Park	FL	http://www.teu.edu

U.S. Career Institute (see US Career Institute)	Degree Granting	Fort Collins	CO	http://www.uscareerinstitute.edu
University of Atlanta	Degree Granting	Atlanta	GA	http://www.uofa.edu
University of Management and Technology	Degree Granting	Arlington	VA	http://www.umtweb.edu
University of Philosophical Research	Degree Granting	Los Angeles	CA	http://www.uprs.edu
University of St. Augustine for Health Sciences (CA)	Degree Granting	San Marcos	CA	http://www.usa.edu
University of St. Augustine for Health Sciences (FL)	Degree Granting	St. Augustine	FL	http://www.usa.edu
US Career Institute (USCI) (a division of Weston Distance Learning)	Degree Granting	Fort Collins	CO	http://www.uscareerinstitute.edu
Western Governors University	Degree Granting	Salt Lake City	UT	http://www.wgu.edu
Westlawn Institute of Marine Technology	Postsecondary	Eastport	ME	http://www.westlawn.edu
William Howard Taft University	Degree Granting	Denver	CO	http://www.taft.edu
World College	Degree Granting	Virginia Beach	VA	http://www.worldcollege.edu
Yorktown University, Inc.	Degree Granting	Denver	CO	http://www.yorktownuniversity.edu

The computer changed everything for Distance Education. Today, we have more schools in DETC than ever before. They span the country and distance is no longer a concern. Telecommunications and internet have changed the way they do business. The western USA is a prime location for DETC schools based on the long distances between urban areas. Telecommunications has truly made travel time almost nothing to some of the sites of the schools who have mastered distance education. Living in a remote area is no longer an inhibitor to a good education if you have electricity and a telephone line for computer communications.

A list of DETC schools follows from the USDE website.

9

UNDERGRADUATES

I taught undergraduates for a long time before I taught graduates. They were mostly younger students seeking their first degrees. I never had a student who was bad. They all had abilities and were working in the real world. The fact that they came to me for computer courses was an improvement in their life. I most of the time taught them from my lesson plans and syllabus. We followed a textbook usually and discussed a lot of the principles in the books. I rarely got off topic. I had a few students who never touched a computer before but these were rare.

The upper level courses were easier to teach since students had some background already. Systems Design was a good course. We went over Life Cycle Management and Project Management in 2 lessons. Could have designed a whole course around that alone. Another good course was Distributed Systems. I taught this many times. We discussed Oracle and other databases that are distributed technologies. The students even programmed some distributed systems. I learned a lot about sockets and communications ports. One student even programmed an RPC call without any help for his project. This was really good stuff.

You have to lead undergraduates to the right answers but not do the work for them. Some of them will act helpless but you must resist helping them. The only way they will gain confidence is to do the projects on their own or in small groups. Small groups are not cheating if you give them time to work in class. They can get ideas from others and work on the problems with help from others. You would not design a class with all small group problems as you need to evaluate each student by themselves also. The small groups will help you prevent from doing the work for the students who are behind or can not do the work at all. You may have to counsel these students to drop the class if it is too hard for them. I have done this several times. I prefer an early drop to a late drop. The late drop may think you are going to solve the problems for them when this is not true.

Most classes are not too bad in the CMIS coursework. You will not have a compiler writing course or a circuit board design course. You may let students build hardware projects using small kits. I found this helpful in several classes. Usually the projects involve some software on a common platform that you have used before. It is not wise to teach courses you have not taken. Students can tell if you have mastered a subject already by your confidence in teaching the class.

10

GRADUATES

Graduate students are very independent and can work alone on projects without too much direction. They need you to advise them but are usually well motivated compared to undergraduate students. They have jobs and are secure in the knowledge that they can do the work required to get another degree. They have good writing skills and are well versed in how to make the grades. Since they need A's and B's they want to do better. Sometimes you have a student who goes onto a PhD degree and you have to give him or her a reference letter. I would do this for most any student who passes my class.

Graduate students are more confident than others. You have to assign them more challenging work. They usually will exceed expectations. Do not lower standards for them. It is the rare graduate student who expects a break in grades. Each graduate student is different and you have to help them independently. You expect more from them so they need to realize this and work more independently. If they go on to doctorate work they will be required to work very independently. You are only the mentor and cannot do the work for them. They will usually come up with original ideas and work independently. You can not ask for more than this at a high quality level. You may also need high quantity in the doctorate program. This requires the student to fully think through his research topic from every angle.

11

TEACHING TO THE TEXTBOOK

In computer sciences the best and worst thing you can do is teach to the textbook. You need concrete examples of software so that throws out the textbook[8]. Some textbooks have software with them but it is not well developed. Software costs so much that the only way they will get exposure is through working on a network at school or on a network at their workplace. My job is to show them various software sets and let them decide what to do next. Unless the class is a programming class and then you must teach them the language in modules. You do this with projects that are harder and harder to complete until you have covered all the different features of the language. This is fun but an open classroom allows you to teach web programming and website building. I try to teach them to use software tools. I have taught MS Project to some of them. These packages have classes that teach just the software. College courses usually teach everything from concept to software.

All textbooks are not equal. Some are very good. Some are poor. If you get to pick a textbook that can be a blessing. You can pick the best book on the subject. I did this for a cyber security course and the result was well planned class sessions with slides from the textbook.

---

[8] Some supplemental texts are very good at Software Engineering. Computer Language courses require these texts.

The students liked the book because they knew it was a kind of reference book[9] for the CISSP certification. They felt comfortable that they could take the exam after the course was over. I do not know how many of them actually did that. Some were just pleased that they finished the class. Most of them were policemen and had never taken a computer course. I taught them in a way that introduced the material and challenged the intermediate and advanced computer users. They had good questions and most of them read the book. They gave me a patch of their unit when the course was done. This was kept by me.

---

[9] Any textbook with the name "Handbook" in the title is a good resource.

12

TEACHING THE SOFTWARE DEVELOPMENT LIFE CYCLE

The Software Development Life Cycle is a guide for your programmers, designers, engineers, testers, and systems analysts. You teach the watershed method, the spiral method, and the iterative method. You show them the validation and verification V model. They begin to see the big picture of how you build a system from beginning to end. Once they realize they do this all the time for different systems they have something of value. It is about patterns and recognizing the next steps before you have to do them. It repeats itself to be successful.

You teach phases or stages as some call them. Feasibility Study, Requirements Analysis, Specifications, Design, Detailed Design, Programming, Testing, Operations and Maintenance. You can show them charts and diagrams. It is really a good thing you have power points on this one.

Watershed Model

The V model is what engineering schools are teaching. They use the V as an acronym for validation and verfication. The V model below is what most colleges use for project management in engineering processes. These processes include software and hardware engineering.

V Model

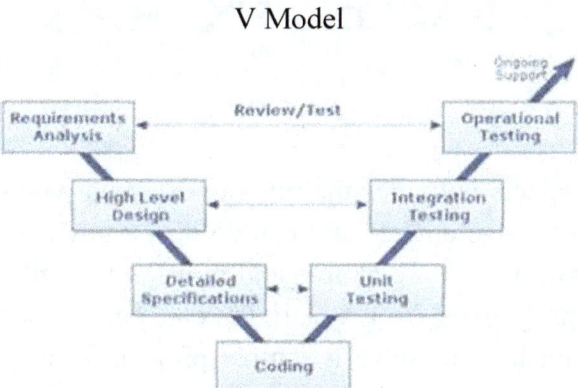

13
TEACHING PROJECTS

Teaching projects is harder than it sounds. What you do is design a project so the average student can do it in a few hours. You start out with projects that are simple and move onto harder projects as the course progresses. You explain the concepts in class and guide them through how to solve a sample project. Then you let them go and solve the project you assigned them. Some people catch on fast. Others see it as a puzzle and like solving puzzles. This is the traditional method of teaching programming at the college level. The student is expected to work on the projects alone without help but that is not always the case. If he turns in copied work then he fails the project. If he turns in work that did not run properly then he also fails the project. You must show inputs, programs, and outputs to get full credit.

Now I am going to tell you two stories on this. In my first programming class on FORTRAN I cruised through all the projects until we hit the quadratic equation project. I went to the dormitory and saw a math major friend of mine and he showed me how to solve the quadratic equation. I then proceeded to solve the FORTRAN project. I did not consider that cheating and I passed the course with an A.

My next computer class was ASSEMBLER Language and we did not write any programs. We read through printouts and understood the language structure and work of registers and commands. This class was good even though we could not program. There was not an ASSEMBLER on the Towson computer which we time shared with. This would hurt me later when I had to write assembler macros on an IBM 370.

In a Simpl-T programming course at Maryland I also went to a friend for our big airline reservation project. There was no way I could finish that project without help. I had a broken ankle and could not get to the computer science center at all in the snow. The teacher was inflexible in my due dates for projects even with a broken ankle. My friend let me copy his program and I changed all the variable names. I turned in the program and got a C in the class. There were 250 students in that class and I knew the teacher would not check each project. He could hardly speak English as Chinese was his first language. This hurt my chances at becoming a pure computer science major but I was glad I passed the class at all.

Shortly after that class I changed my major to business computing. There I took 2 COBOL classes and some MIS courses. The first COBOL class had 10 projects. They were all easy enough to finish on my own since I had some previous experience with FORTRAN, Assembler, and SIMPL-T. So I knew I was in the right place. The MIS classes talked about information theory in organizations. Dr. Kirchberg was great at discussions. Again I knew I could do this more easily than computer sciences from a practical viewpoint. They actually explained how to use information in management. I enjoyed the management part of the equation. Years later I went for a degree in Organizational Management online.

My Urban Planning classes required programming census data in SPSS. Statistical Package for Social Sciences. I was so good in this that my teacher hired me for a special programming project. She knew I was an IFSM and Computer guy. I got an A on the project.

I was good at writing up the interpretation of data points in SPSS. I could tell you what all the stats meant.

The 2nd COBOL class was Advanced COBOL. We had to do several projects for this class also building on what we learned in the first COBOL class. I enjoyed the classes and decided I wanted a job as a COBOL programmer. I also took a Systems Analysis course at Maryland where we learned PSL/PSA. I found a programming job at Navy Medical Data Services Center and I worked there 10 years. I started as an intern and then worked there permanently. I had to learn JCL and this was easy enough. I found a good COBOL book and used it to model the programs I was writing for Uncle Sam. You see it is all about patterns. There is a pattern for every system and every program you ever write that is repeatable. A good book will show you this. I learned Interactive COBOL and ADAMINT Calls and rewrote the BUMIS system – a Navy personnel system.

After 5 years I moved to the database division and learned NATURAL and ADABAS. NATURAL is like FORTRAN and COBOL together in one language. When we taught NATURAL we broke down the projects so Navy Officers could do the programming. They caught on very fast and soon we had User Programmed Reports. I created a system of User Reports and called it the Public System. Got a $1000 bonus for that one. Any end user could run the programs after they selected it from the list. This was revolutionary because normal people were now programming. We changed the culture of Navy Medical to an ADABAS/NATURAL corporate database from COBOL written by only programmers. Some of the officers became liaisons to us and taught our courses to others. Some were very good at logical thinking and programming. They made good students.

In computer sciences you must learn through the projects you do. In graduate school I learned a good lesson about programming in too many languages at once. I took a programming class and it required programs in multiple languages. Some of them I had no experience with at all like PL/1 and ALGOL. I was suppose to write the programs and compare the run times and outputs to each other. I had a hard time doing that and got a D in the class. It was my only D in my academic career but I learned a good lesson about programming. Do not think you know it all because you will meet projects that will kick your butt. I switched over into MIS and only programmed in DBASE II and III after that experience for my database class. Got an A in that course. Had a semester project I delivered to the instructor on a Kaypro laptop. It was a nice system for student grading. That was a great project and I used it for myself years later.

What I learned was that I had a problem with the compact languages like C and C++. The database languages were always easier for me. GW BASIC was easy to learn but I had a hard time with Visual BASIC. RBASE 5000 was easy. All the packages were easy. I do not think I was lazy just did not have enough talent in compact languages. I can write some Javascript and HTML and XML are easy. Other languages like PASCAL and TURBO C are not so easy for me. Just don't make the connections all the time. I should be able to pick them up better but have never had a class in C. This is an oversight for an old mainframe programmer. No good micro PC programmer would let this happen.

Spreadsheets and databases and work processors are easy for me. MS Project and Microstation are easy. Cyber tools are easy for me. These make good projects in cyber classes. You will know the students who like programming because they will show you results. It is up to you to help them improve their skill set based on your advanced skill set. In this regard teaching programming is harder than teaching other subjects and you have to have great experience with many software languages and packages.

You have to regress and have skills at problem solving in a group environment often a computer lab. This can be easy for some people or hard for others. You will answer questions as you go through a lab session and that may be enough for most students. Other students may answer questions you do not know. Never lie to a student if you do not know an answer. Tell them you will research the answer and find out by next session.

14

TRACE OF COURSES

The following table shows the order I took my computer courses and when I took them. This might help with advising students on taking computer classes in a sequence. I took many classes as I began to understand computers better. I switched from computer science to MIS and took more managerial classes as I moved up the chain of command. The more software projects I wrote and delivered the higher I went in the food chain. Today, I write papers and books and the occasional software system or CDROM system.

1975	FORTRAN	UNIVAC	St Mary's College
1976	ASSEMBLER	No Computer	St Mary's College
1976	Statistics	No Computer	St Mary's College
1977	SiMPL-T	UNIVAC 1106[10]	Univ. Maryland
1977	Discrete Structures[11]	UNIVAC 1106	Univ. Maryland
1978	COBOL I & EXEC 8	UNIVAC 1106	Univ. Maryland
1978	Computers in Society IFSM 201	No computer	Univ. Maryland
1978	SPSS	UNIVAC 1108	Univ. Maryland
1978	COBOL II	UNIVAC 1108	Univ. Maryland

---

[10] Required mastery of IBM Card Punch 29 for card decks of programs.
[11] Withdrew from this course when I could not understand the teacher from India. This too helped me decide to go to IFSM Business Computing from a Computer Sciences major.

1978	MIS Theory IFSM 301	No Computer	Univ. Maryland
1979	Advanced COBOL & JCL	IBM 370	NIH DCTR
1979	Systems Analysis – PSL/PSA	UNIVAC 1108	Univ. Maryland
1979	SAS	IBM 360	Navy Medical
1979	TSO CLISTS	IBM 360	Navy Medical
1980	Project Management	No Computer	US Navy – DOD CI
1981	ADABAS	IBM 370	Software AG.
1982	Real Time Systems		American Univ.
1982	Direct Calls ADAMINT	IBM 370	Software AG
1983	NATURAL	IBM 370	Software AG
1983	Systems Approach		American Univ.
1984	ADABAS Performance & Tuning	IBM 370	Software AG
1984	Databases		American Univ.
1984	Computer Security		American Univ.
1985	GW BASIC	IBM PC	Self Taught
1985	Telecommunications		American Univ.
1986	MS Project	IBM PC	Self Taught
1986	MVS	IBM 370	Navy Medical
1986	MVS Utilities	IBM 370	Marines Corps
1987	Genifer Code Generator	IBM PC	Navy Medical
1987	ORACLE 7	VAX VMS	Self Taught
1988	CLIPPER	IBM PC	Self Taught
1986	RDBMS – Dbase III	IBM PC	American Univ.
1986	Systems Design	IBM PC	American Univ.
1986	Reporting Systems	IBM PC	American Univ.
1987	Quant. Analysis	IBM PC	American Univ.
1987	Managerial Economics	IBM PC	American Univ.
1988	MS Technology Mgt		American Univ.
1992	NETWARE 386	IBM PC	Kramer Systems
1993	HTML	IBM PC	GSA
1994	DBASE IV	IBM PC	GSA
1994	TQM	IBM PC	GSA
1995	MS Office	IBM PC	Self Taught

1996	Contract Management	MS Certificate	George Washington Univ.
1997	ORACLE 8	IBM PC	Learning Tree
1997	PL/SQL	IBM PC	CSC
1998	MS Access	IBM PC	SHA
2001	IDEFX, ERWIN	IBM PC	KWU
2001	Artificial Intelligence	IBM PC	KWU
2001	Object Oriented	IBM PC	KWU
2001	Stats For Mgrs – Minitab	IBM PC	KWU
2001	PhD MIS		KWU
2004	CISM & CDMP		Certifications
2006	Microstation	IBM PC	Self Taught
2007	SENTINEL cybertools	IBM PC	Univ Arkansas
2009	BA – Organizational Management	Degree	Ashford Univ.
2010	ITS RDBMS	IBM PC	Maryland Eng.
2010	ITS Telecomm	IBM PC	Maryland Eng.
2010	Systems Engineering	IBM PC	Maryland Eng.
2011	Cyber courses	IBM PC	DHS

I am always learning more. Am not programming as much as I once did but I do more managerial duties now like contract management and project management. Most of my classes were just-in-time classes and I used what I learned immediately. I progressed at a slow rate through some degree programs in order to perform better at work and absorb the new languages and technologies. I never felt I was totally on top of all the technologies to be a great programmer. There were always new languages to learn because of the work projects to be done. In this regard training was required before the work could be done.

When I came to state government I continued to train in programming languages and databases. I have studied operating systems on my own time. I usually buy a good book on the one I am using. I have retrained several times now and reinvented myself. I had to do this for Homeland Security and Emergency Management which I did not list in the table. It was fun and I enjoyed the classes.

Now I am embarking on an MBA program in Project Management. This should be a natural direction for me at this age. I can use the business sense and PM training at work once again.

15

A SAMPLE SYLLABUS TEMPLATE

This chapter discusses a sample syllabus for the computer sciences college teacher. The syllabus is similar to a standard course except for the projects assigned. There may be more than one project and you need to have deadline dates and expectations for each project listed in the syllabus. Following is a sample syllabus from Concord University[12] – an online law school in California.

CONCORD 101 - Syllabus Template
[replace w/Course identifiers]

> [Feel free to use any of the content in this syllabus for your own syllabi. There are hints (identified by brackets []) which suggest the *type* of content to enter according to your personal preferences. There is also content which is *required* in all syllabi for online courses. These sections are identified with an asterisk *. Please contact Jennifer Humphries with questions or concerns.]
> Contact Information
> Phone: 304-384-6265
> Email: jhumphries@cat.concord.edu

---

[12] Accredited Law School but no formal classes for learning trials.

Credit Hours: 3 credit hours
Prerequisites: None
Instructor:
Dr. Polly Ester
Home: 304-555-6450 from 6PM to 10 PM
Office: 304-384- ext 1428 from 8AM to 5PM
Email: pester@concord.edu
Course Description:
[Catalog course description goes here.]
Course Text:
[Text Title]
ISBN# xxxxxxxxxxx
Available in the CU Bookstore.
Course Learning Goals and Objectives:
During this course the student will:

- Objective #1
- Objective #2
- Objective #3
- Objective #4
- Objective #5

Evaluation: [EVALUATION DESCRIPTION GOES HERE. Feel free to replace any existing text with your own content unless otherwise indicated with an asterisk.]
Evaluation is based on the average of xxxxxxxxxxxxxxxxxxxxxxxxxxxxxxxxxxx.

Grades will be posted within seven days of the assignment deadline. Please note that grades will only be posted in Blackboard or Ellie within the confines of a password protected environment.

Late work will not be tolerated. The deadlines for each assignment are absolute. Any assignment that is received late for any amount of time (even a few minutes) will not be examined by the instructor nor will it obtain credit. Technological trouble (i.e. computer or internet problems) is not an acceptable excuse for late work. It is highly recommended that students back up all work, including discussion posts. In the event that a technological problem arises, students may email work directly to me *by the deadline*.

Grading Scale: [use preferred grading scale]

90-100	A
80-89	B
70-79	C
60-69	D
0-59	F

Course Outline:
[insert course outline here]
Examinations: [insert personal exam preferences]
Exams will be multiple choice consisting of 20 questions.

*Tests in this class are all electronic.
Assignments:
[replace with personal assignment preferences] Work every other odd problem....1,5,9....... SHOW ALL WORK

*Assignments during this course should be submitted using the Blackboard Assignment Drop Box. All assignments must be saved as Microsoft Word 97-2003 documents (.doc) and saved with an assignment-specific description and your initials. For example John Howard may save as "assignment1JH.doc". See error from www.reddit.com.

Participation: [replace with personal discussion preferences, if any]
Join the class discussions frequently. I'll post one discussion question per week. In turn, all students will be required to:

1. Post one answer to the weekly question (due every Wednesday by 11:55 p.m.).
2. Respond to a total of two of your classmates' (by Friday 11:55 p.m.).
3. Read all of the postings each week.

Please note that all posts should add something significant to the topic at hand. You should avoid posts that simply compliment (e.g. "Interesting post!") or support (e.g. "I agree with you.") another student's work; you will not be given credit for these sorts of comments.

When attempting to communicate online, it can be easy to overlook the fact that you're talking in black and white ink or in a public discussion. Though I expect to have lively discussions in this course, personal attacks on another student of any kind is not acceptable. Students who engage in personal attacks will be subject to one of two courses of action:

1. a score of zero for the week's discussion for the first offense
2. a letter grade of "F" and/or dismissal from the class for repeated offenses.

If you have an issue with a classmate, please contact the instructor immediately. Do not confront the other student directly.

COURSE POLICIES:
***Plagiarism & Academic Dishonesty*:** *Plagiarism is stealing or passing off as one's own, ideas or words of another, whether or not copyrighted. Plagiarism will be penalized by the instructor according to the degree of dishonesty the instructor judges is involved. Students guilty of academic dishonesty are subject to disciplinary action. Disciplinary action may include, but is not limited to: reduction of a grade on an assignment or examination,

reduction of a grade for the class, suspension or expulsion from the University. Students may appeal disciplinary action taken against them by filing a grievance.

NOTE : It is YOUR responsibility to keep a copy of ALL your work. Also, keep a backup copy of any course work completed on a computer. CU will not be responsible for any loss of materials.

Americans with Disabilities Act Standards: *Concord University is committed to responding to the needs of students with disabilities as defined by the Americans with Disabilities Act. Students who request academic accommodations or modifications related to a disability should first notify their instructor and then contact the Vice President and Academic Dean's Office.

Withdrawal from the course: [include policies for withdrawal]

*Required syllabus content for course delivered 100% online.

© 2009 Concord University

16

A SAMPLE RESEARCH PAPER TEMPLATE

Computer science people need to know how to write effectively. They will be writing technical documents and papers and need to know how to research as good as anyone else. It is not enough to just be a good programmer. You have to be a communicator to lead teams of programmers[13].

The structure of research paper outline template is listed in the following example template. It is very important to choose appropriate template. Make sure it meets all the requirements of the research paper. The essential **research paper outline template** would look like this:

Introduction:

- Introduction of the topic
- Examination of the problem
- Location of the background
- Posing the thesis

---

[13] This can be done through writing technical details down and project plans.

Body paragraph-1:

- Link to the Introduction
- Discussion of the object in detail
- Expression of your opinion on the concern

Body paragraph-2:

- Fluent transition to the main point of polemic
- Particularized discussion with appropriate examples and cited sources
- Completion of discussion point

Body paragraphs-3, 4 and 5:

- Discussion of each point with necessary adjustments where they are needed
- Link to the final body paragraph

Conclusion:

- Renovation of the thesis
- Summarizing of the main points
- Conclusion discussion. Positive announcement of successful accomplishment of research

Use this template as you see fit. Maybe you could hand it out to freshmen students only. Maybe you could go over it on the board like I do. It is a good resource to have in your bag of tricks.

17

GRADING ONLINE

Grading online is easy when you have internet email and access to websites. The students can contact you directly or you can post the grades for them on the website. They usually do not argue the grades. You should provide explanations for lower grades. Evidence of understanding is the primary content you are looking for. If there is no evidence of this then you can give the lower grade. Most students answer the questions straight forwardly. Very few will give live examples using their workplace. I know that students do not write very well so I tell them what to look for when they are doing a paper.

Good writers keep you informed and know how to tell a story. They present a body of data and evidence for their hypothesis and show you why they think a certain way. This is called the scientific method and has been around a while in college writing. If they just ramble on then I give them a lower grade. If they prove a point then I grade higher.

Tests and exams have specific answers and are not hard to grade. An answer key helps you do this. I never try to grade papers relative to each other but I am conscious about how many A's I give out. I give out more B's and C's. The writer really has to impress me that he knows what he is talking about. Good grammar always helps. I am no English Teacher but I know you should be able to write the King's English if you are in college. A remedial writing course may be the most useful to college students starting out on the college journey. I have never figured out why they are not tested for writing abilities when they start their college experience. This seems like a logical reason to test for abilities before they reach the harder courses where writing is more demanding.

It is hard for student who does not know how to write well adapt as he goes through a program of courses. Much easier to take him aside in the start of the program and help him improve his/her writing abilities.

18

EVALUATING PROGRAMS

How can you evaluate a program at a school? You need to look at all the courses and teachers and decide if you want to take these courses. Will they improve you when you are finished? Or are they a repeat of what you already know? If you are teaching and leading a department you need to annually evaluate your programs of instruction for relevancy and currency. Technology courses can become outdated fast. You need to be aware of what your staff is teaching. Use student evaluations of instructors to gauge where the program is at this time. Things change and you must adapt or be left behind. You do not want a college computer science program that is obsolete.

Keep on the lookout for new technologies and new ideas in addition to old hat ideas that have worked before. Test new ideas and see if they hold water. Develop your own courses to become a great teacher while you are still an administrator. This will keep you in practice and prevent you from being far from the teachers. They will truly admire you for teaching while you administer. Give adjuncts new assignments and make sure they have many years under their belts before promoting them to full time. This should be the rare case.

Adjuncts know they are not going to be paid full price. They teach because they love the teaching and respect they get back. The money has nothing to do with it but as an extra income source. Most teachers know they are going to be paid less than other professions.

19

STUDENT EVALUATIONS

You have to evaluate each student on participation, assignments, tests, papers, projects, and exams. There is no way to tell if the students learned a lot or a little in your class other than by the grades they are given. Students would rather have more projects and a paper than take tests. You have to give them a chance to make grades in several different ways. This way if a person is a bad test taker they have a chance to score on the projects and paper. You will tell if the effort is there.

Systematic ways of evaluating students include blackboard and any systems you create to track grades. I created a Student Evaluation System in Clipper in 1993 and used it in classes until I taught using blackboard. Never did give it to anyone but it came in real handy. It automatically computed means and grade point averages. It was an excellent system for the teacher to use. Should have sold it to someone who could distribute it but never got around to that. Instead, I put a copy in my desk drawer at home where it remains.

Never have your students rate you on the same day that you rate them. This is not a good practice. Some students will retaliate with poor ratings because you rated them lower than they expected. Give them the chance to rate you before you rate them. This will ensure that there is no retaliation in ratings. Also tell them that the ratings will be used for future class assignments even if this is not true. Full disclosure is a good idea if they enjoyed your class. This holds you accountable.

20
THE GREATEST TEACHERS

Who were the greatest teachers of all time across all boundaries? Jesus, Moses, Solomon, Mohammed, Buddah, Confusious, Pythagoras, Socrates, Plato, Albert Einstein, Richard Feynman, Donald Knuth, Grace Hopper? This question is highly debatable and depends on your perspective. A quality of a great teacher is that he can reach the masses and he simplifies his ideas. Every one in this list can do that. A great teacher must also create a structure to continue his work. A great teacher teaches after he is gone and continues to teach through the ages.

We can break down the teachers in this list by religious teachers, philosophy teachers, math teachers, physics teachers, and computer science teachers. We all have something from each of them. As computer science teachers we emulate the best of each of them. It is not enough to just use computer science theory and examples in great teaching. Math axioms are very similar to theological parables. Religions have rules and laws and math has rules and laws. Computer sciences also has rules and laws. It is a modern science to be sure but not so much different than those of the past. It is based on electronics a fairly new science but conforms to math. Surely Pythagoras had ideas on Geometry that can be used today in building of any architecture and computerized drawings. This is knowledge that has bridged the ages. The Golden Ratio is everywhere we look in life. Computerized CADD drawings of the modern world could not exist without geometry.

Richard Feynman was a great physics teacher at Cal Tech. They preserved his lectures on videotape. He was the best of those who served on the Atom Bomb Manhatten Project in World War II. He had the idea that he could make physics simple for the every day college student. One of his books was called <u>Seven Easy Pieces</u>. This referred to physics and the 7 parts he thought were most important. It is a truly masterful book.

Donald Knuth must be one of the greatest computer science teachers of all time. His book <u>The Art of Computer Programming</u> gave us much information and is used today as a guide. I would also say Grace Hopper was a great teacher of computer science. She was living history since she was involved in the first computer at Harvard. See my notes in the next chapter on the best Adjunct teacher I ever had.

Who would be the greatest teacher of all time? Would it be God? He gave us everything we know, sense, and feel. He gave us Jesus, his son. He created more than we know in the universe. I would suggest there is none greater than he. Jesus was a great teacher also. It is hard to distinguish where God starts and stops with Jesus. Most of his teachings were inspired by the Devine. How do we not place him as the number one teacher of all time across all cultures and nations?

21
ADJUNCT FOREVER?

The best adjunct teacher I ever knew was Col. RJ Tufts. He was my database instructor at American University. He worked at Andrews AFB Systems Command and invited me there to deliver a project paper I worked on. I was working at Bethesda Navy Medical at the time. Col. Tufts was a DBA Supervisor. I wrote about ADABAS and how Navy Medical used it when I was on staff there. I think he liked me. He told me there might be an opening at Systems Command. He actually wrote a chapter in the Richard Bassler textbook on databases. Col Tufts was published by the Air Force Academy also. He took his class to lunch at Fort McNair Officers Club at the end of the semester. He had a great impact on me since I attended USAFA in 1974. I never told him.

It's not bad to be an adjunct forever if you remember them the way I remember RJ Tufts. He was no-nonsense and really smart. He helped me understand database technology from the inside out. I had already been through the ADABAS courses with Software AG so I knew the inverted databases but I had no experience with relational databases. I got that experience with Dr. Bassler's microcomputer databases course. If I could be half as good as Col Tufts I would take it. He was the total government DBA package. Even my boss had far to go to beat RJ Tufts.

I never was an Air Force Colonel but I saw some of what I learned at the academy in Col Tufts. Ethics and integrity were his specialty. He was a good teacher and he knew his stuff well. He must have been on staff for a while because Dr. Bassler used his article in his 1976 book on database technology. By the time I was there it was 1984. I was not on staff at UMUC yet but was getting there. I was halfway through my courses at American.

If I could be a tenured professor I would do it in a heartbeat. But then I would lose my civil service job. This would not be good. So in retrospect being an adjunct for life might not be bad if I could be as good as Col Tufts. I get to try that every time I write a new book. My future writings are not limited to just technology. This helps me stay sharp while I am not in the classroom.

Who would I learn from in the corporate world? Oracle CEO Larry Ellison grows his company by acquiring related companies. He is a no nonsense guy. He was once a computer programmer who wanted his own company. He became wise in stock investments and built an empire. Oracle is one of the better software companies with a real product of value in Relational Oracle. How would you like to learn from him? You would have to learn to be a business shark.

Larry Ellison – Oracle CEO

22

JOB HUNTING

When you have a civil service job you don't have to job hunt. The jobs come to you. Everyone knows when new jobs are posted. Bosses have a good idea of who they will select. Adjunct faculty know it only takes an interview to gain employment. After the interview you will know if you can rely on that school to help you teach. The person hiring will tell you. Adjuncts get classes that other teachers do not want. The night classes and remote classes. You get used to doing whatever it takes.

I have my standards now that I have taught graduate school. I have thought about administration but I am not full time in the education business. I could transition if I got the right job at the right school close to home. There are only a few of these near where I live. Once you have experience you just do not want to take any job. It has to be challenging and it has to be local. You can not be traveling to other states to deliver a class unless you have the time and money for gas. I tried this at George Washington and it was a long drive to Alexandria. No parking. No extra cash for traveling 85 miles roundtrip.

I look for jobs on Chronicles of Higher Education before the semester starts. This is always the best time to interview If you make an impression you will get the job. You have to be straight forward and know you may only teach there one time but you interview anyway like you will be there for 25 classes. Self confidence works wonders at these interviews. If you know some of the staff already then that is good. Never act like you have the job and be humble. A good adjunct is always humble because he may not have a job next semester if enrollment goes down.

You should always be open to new jobs in teaching because you never know what you will learn. Each assignment I have taken has been different and new. Some were even similar to previous assignments but all were unique because the students were different. Over the years the technologies have changed somewhat and new companies are using newer technologies that you have to stay up with. The basics never change. By being an adjunct you are closer to the knowledge factory that is our college system. You are in the know when it comes to latest developments. You can be proud of that. You can always be sure that some student will think he is smarter than you and will inform you when you are wrong.

I have found that leaving resumes for call backs does not usually work that well. You have to get an interview as soon as you can to beat the competition. The call back method only works if you know the school or have already taught there before and they have a file on you.

Once you reach a certain age and do not have the energy any more you may want to slow down. Just remember that everything is a learning experience. If you slow down you may not live too long.

23

FLEXIBILITY

It pays to remain flexible during your teaching career. My kids have taught me that no matter how much I learn the next generation will come along and think they know more. This is because they do. Knowledge doubles every seven years. Kids today are asked to know a lot more than we were. They have abilities because they have more complex toys and better teachers than we had. They will almost always do things instinctively in technology where we were not trained at all.

You should be able to teach within a few days and you should try teaching at remote sites. Never refuse to teach unless you have a good reason. The main thing is trying to get the information to the students and planning your course. Writing the syllabus is critical in this task. If you are lucky enough to use Blackboard and select your textbook use caution. Make sure you give plenty of information to the students and plan for their well being after the class. If they want to take a certification test after the class then help them learn enough to do that. You have to ask your hiring official how he wants you to approach the class you teach. If they leave it all up to you then error on the side of too much information rather than too little.

You took classes a long time ago and the knowledge may have changed since then. Some of it may have been updated. Preview every book you use in the courses even if you do not select them.

Sometimes you have no choice. But you have to be well prepared. Planning is 99% of success in college courses. Going off the cuff is hardly ever successful unless it is in lab class where you can do that effectively and demonstrate juicy software and programming skills.

24
ADJUNCT BENEFITS

The greatest benefit is helping people learn more. You also learn leadership by teaching as adjunct faculty. You get face time with new people in the field of computers. You keep learning even as a teacher. You gain confidence in your knowledge about computer sciences by teaching others. You see an all new perspective.

Lord knows you won't make a lot of money. You could spend your time worse. You might even become a writer and author in the process like I did. Now I look forward to writing another book like teaching a new class. My books do not sell a lot but I know I am helping others.

It is too bad that colleges do not issue stock. Then we could invest in them like companies and watch them grow. Instead they invest in human capital – the students. They increase knowledge and personal growth. How do we measure this using money? Almost impossible unless we look at salaries of graduates versus salaries of non- graduates. We know college educations are valuable because salary data tells us this is true. In companies, executives value the staff with degrees enough to pay them for it. Will a person with 3 degrees get more than a person with one degree? Maybe. We do know that learning is ongoing and never stops even as we die.

A good adjunct learns that he has value beyond the money he earns. He learns that helping the students has it's own rewards and he will grow from this. It will make him a better leader. I do not know anyone who can not benefit from public speaking and teaching required by a computer science course.

25

FINAL THOUGHTS

If anyone reading this has decided to become an adjunct faculty member then I congratulate you. For the rest of you I hope your journey is nice. May you keep on learning and applying what you know. Man's Flight Through Life is Powered by His Knowledge – USAFA Eagle Statue in Air Gardens. My hope is that you keep on learning and growing by however you best learn. Learn by doing or learn by reading. Do more to enhance your learning in the future. Go back for another degree or simply take some classes on your own. You can find plenty of free classes online today.

Computer learning is the way of the future. You should try to take at least one course in this format and you might be surprised how you do. My kids have all mastered this approach and they now know they have computers kills that are pretty good. They could even teach online if they wanted to. Distance education has been revolutionized by the micro-computer and telecommunications. Never again will a major segment of our rural population be left out of the education market.

Computer sciences is based on trial and error or writing software and inspecting the results. As long as the scientific method is alive computer scientists will be needed to create new software and hardware. The US Patent office plays an important role in the guidance of this business even though software is not patented but copyrighted.

When you create new software you are experiencing trial and error processing of data. To have a method of software development helps us control our outputs better and our time.

The time invested in programming is sometimes long and hard. The payout is usually good and the sense of achievement can make you proud. In every job where you create something new you are manufacturing a new product. Software is no different. There is a lot of money in new ideas and putting these ideas online. We have seen the DOT COM revolution and websites become worth millions of dollars (like Amazon). How can computer sciences grow effectively in the future to handle all the new ideas? This is an evolving science as the capabilities of machines improves and chips become stronger and smarter. There is no real limit even using Moore's Law applied to the life cycle of computer systems. There are a number of secret projects to use computers for many different functions by the government. When you consider that embedded computers can have a great impact in electronic weapons systems you understand why this is true. In fact, there is a whole area of cyber security dedicated to cyberwarfare. This could in fact happen today in the world of computers.

We need to be vigilant and impress upon our students that anything can be used for evil if we let it. It is our moral obligation as teachers to make sure we teach that cyber security is to be used for good not evil. By applying moral conduct to our students we will make a great future for all computer scientists. One day we will have congressmen who are computer scientists.

26
BIBLIOGRAPHY

Bassler & Logan, (1976), <u>The Technology of Data Base Management Systems</u>, 3rd Edition, College Readings, Inc, Alexandria, VA.

Booch, Grady & Bryan, Doug, (1994), <u>Software Engineering with ADA</u>, 3rd Edition, Benjamin Cummings Publishing company, Redwood, CA.

Date, CJ, (1995), <u>An Introduction to Database Systems</u>, 6th Edition, Addison Wesley Publishing Company, Reading, Mass

Heinze, David, (1982), <u>Management Science Introductory Concepts and Applications</u>, Southwestern Publishing, Cincinnati, OH.

Kroenke, David (1977), <u>Database Processing Fundamentals, Modeling, Applications</u>, Science Research Associates, Chicago.

Stallings, William (2009), <u>Business Data Communications</u>, Pearson Prentice Hall, Upper Saddle, NJ.

Stone, F, (2002), <u>The Oracle of Oracle</u>, AMACOM, American Management Association, New York.

Tanenbaum, Andrew, (1981), <u>Computer Networks</u>, Prentice Hall, Englewood, NJ.

27

BIOGRAPHY

Donald Joseph Gray Chiarella lives in Elkridge-Hanover in Howard County, Maryland with his wife Mimi, a master teacher, and 4 great children. Born in Kilmarnock, Scotland in 1956 to a US Air Force family, eldest son of Donald Sr. and Margaret. He is CEO and President of Chiarella Consulting. Don was a Homeland Security Manager in the Motor Carrier Division of Maryland SHA and was with the State of Maryland for 20 years. He was previously the MIS Section Chief for Maryland State Highway Administration in the Traffic Safety Analysis Division from 1997-2005. He retired in 2018 from SHA. He retired from Federal GSA in 1997 with 18 years of service. He won the 2018 Marquis Lifetime Achievement Award. He holds an independent study online Ph.D. from Kennedy-Western University in MIS (2001) an M.S. degree in Technology of Management from American University (1988) (Dean's List), and a B.A. degree in Urban Planning / IFSM from University of Maryland (1979) with the first degree in those two specialties. He also holds a second online bachelor's degree from Ashford University in Organizational Management (2009) where he made the Dean's list. He holds an MBA in Project Management from Aspen University (2016). He is certified by George Washington University Law School in Public Contracts Management. He is also certified by the ICCP and DAMA as a Certified Data Management Professional (CDMP). He is a Certified Information Security Manager by ISACA (CISM). He is certified by University of Maryland Clark Engineering School in Traffic Engineering. He holds the CPEM certification from ASEM. He has attended the Naval Post Graduate School, National Defense University, Department of Defense Computer Institute, and US Air Force Academy without graduating. Previously, he worked for the US Navy Medical Data Services Center at Bethesda and GSA Central Office in Washington DC before retiring from Federal Civil Service. He is a 1974 Nixon presidential and 1975 Maryland state scholarship winner and has won a college championship in baseball (catcher) in the PIC NAIA Conference in 1976 at St. Mary's College of Maryland. He is ASEP coaching certified and served as a little league commissioner for the Upper Marlboro Boys and Girls Club in basketball in 1987. He won an award for staff mentoring from GSA in 1994. He is a life member of the US Naval Institute, AFCEA, American University Alumni, and USAF Academy Association of Graduates. Don has built over 20 computer systems including webpages, CDROMS, and management software and written many papers and documents for government systems management and planning and the private sector. He has studied 4 foreign languages and more than 10 computer languages, 7 operating systems, and 5 databases. He was a Democratic Chief Voting Judge in Howard County. He was also on staff at George Washington University recently. He is a 32nd degree Mason and President of Glen Mar United Methodist Men. He has taught over 35 courses and written 25 books over the years some of which are available at www.lulu.com/donchiarella. His favorite authors are Ernest Hemmingway and Ray Bradbury. He enjoys travel, sports, motor cycling, coin collecting, and family time with the kids, grandkids, and wife. He is a Washington Redskins, Nationals, Wizards, and Capitals fan. He is also a Knight Templar Mason in Maryland since 2011 and Trustee at Glen Mar United Methodist Church in Ellicott City, Maryland.

www.ingramcontent.com/pod-product-compliance
Lightning Source LLC
LaVergne TN
LVHW021944060526
838200LV00042B/1922